All the pages in ... —in Japanese RIGHT-t... d or altered, so you can ... hem to be read.

FLIP IT!

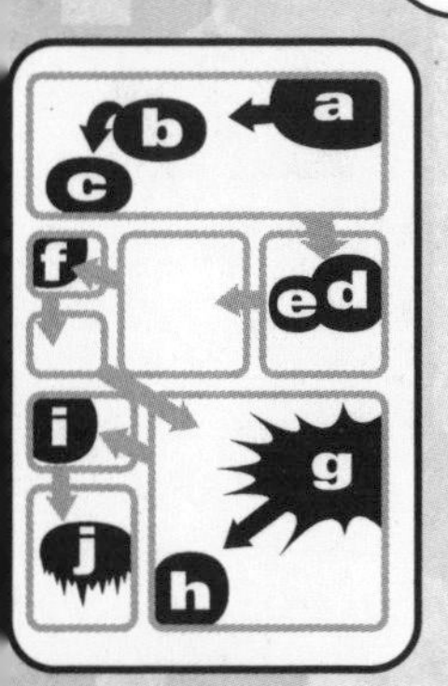

RIGHT TO LEFT?!

Traditional Japanese manga starts at the upper right-hand corner, and moves right-to-left as it goes down the page. Follow this guide for an easy understanding.

For more information and sneak previews, visit cmxmanga.com. Call 1-888-COMIC BOOK for the nearest comics shop or head to your local book store.

This book is manufactured at a facility holding chain-of-custody certification.
This paper is made with sustainably managed North American fiber.

DC Comics, a Warner Bros. Entertainment Company.

Alethea & Athena Nibley – Translation and Adaptation
MPS Ad Studio – Lettering
Larry Berry – Design
Sarah Farber – Assistant Editor
Jim Chadwick – Editor

SUSTAINABLE FORESTRY INITIATIVE Certified Fiber Sourcing www.sfiprogram.org PWC-SFICOC-260

ISBN: 978-1-4012-1598-9

THE NAME OF THE FLOWER, CHAPTER 15 / END

...YOUR MOTHER WAS A WONDERFUL PERSON...
WASN'T SHE?
...
YES...

SHE LET IS SLIP THAT...
"IT WAS A ONCE-IN-A-LIFETIME ROMANCE...
...THAT WOULD NEVER COME TRUE."
SHE WAS TOYED WITH BY FATE...
BUT EVEN SO...
SHE WAS GRACE-FULLY STRONG.
THAT'S THE KIND OF WOMAN YOUR MOTHER WAS...
ACCORD-ING TO YOH.
IT MUST HAVE BEEN HARD TO PASS ON, LEAVING HER CHILD BEHIND.
BUT I HAVE NO DOUBT THAT SHE'S WATCHING FROM HEAVEN, AND SMILING...
...AT WHAT A FINE YOUNG MAN YOU'VE BECOME.

ONCE, HE AND SAKURA GOT INTO A BIG FIGHT BECAUSE...
...HE TOLD HER HE TRIED TO GIVE THEIR ENTIRE SAVINGS, WHICH WEREN'T MUCH...
...TO YOUR MOTHER, NAGISA-SAN.
I CAN SEE IT...
BUT, WELL...
SHE TURNED HIM DOWN FLAT.
SHE SAID, "I'LL PROTECT MY CHILD MYSELF.
I WANT YOU TO WATCH OVER US."
YOH LAUGHED ABOUT HOW SHE QUIETLY GOT MAD AT HIM.
SHE WAS SO MILD-MANNERED...
BUT WHEN IT CAME TO YOU...
SHE WAS STUBBORN AND WOULD NOT BACK DOWN.
APPARENTLY SHE NEVER SAID A WORD ABOUT THE KATAOKA HOUSEHOLD.
BUT JUST ONCE...
SHE MENTIONED FUJIYA-SAN.

YOU DO RESEMBLE ... FUJIYA KATAOKA-SAN.
YOU KNOW MY GRAND-FATHER?
Ha ha
THERE AREN'T MANY IN MY GENERATION WHO *DON'T* KNOW FUJIYA KATAOKA-SAN.
HE WAS A GREAT MAN WHO LOST HIS WIFE AT A YOUNG AGE AND BUILT THE KATAOKA ZAIBATSU FROM SCRATCH.
HE HAD A SOLID REPUTATION FOR BEING A WONDERFUL MAN OF CHARACTER.
AND I HAVE A GENERAL IDEA OF YOUR CIRCUM-STANCES...
FROM WHAT YOH TOLD ME.
YOH ...
HE WAS THOUGHTLESS, INCREDIBLY SOFT-HEARTED, A MORON THROUGH AND THROUGH, AND HE HAD A WEAKNESS FOR BEAUTIES.
THAT IDIOT.

CHOUKO.
HELLO, GRANDPA.
UM...
THIS IS KEI MIZUSHIMA-SAN...
THE MAN I'VE BEEN STAYING WITH.
...I'M PLEASED TO MEET YOU.
OH,
IT'S ...
"KEI-KUN."
SHOCK!
...
?
YOU KNOW HIM...?
NO, NO.
THIS IS THE FIRST TIME WE'VE MET.
BUT...
...WHEN YOH CAME BACK FROM KYOTO...
...YOU'RE ALL HE EVER TALKED ABOUT.
OH,
IT'S TRUE.

I REALLY AM GLAD...
...THAT YOU'RE HERE, AKIYAMA-SAN.
THANK YOU VERY MUCH.
Chou!
AH,
COMING!
PATTER PATTER

...DO YOU REMEMBER...
BEFORE, WHEN I SAID YOU'RE A LITTLE LIKE MY FATHER...?
MY FATHER WAS HAPPY AND FUN,
A BOTTOMLESS PIT OF CHEERFULNESS.
HE SEEMED LIKE HE WASN'T ALL THERE, BUT SOMETIMES HE WOULD SAY VERY PERCEPTIVE THINGS. YOU COULD NEVER TELL WHAT HE WAS THINKING.
HE WAS LIKE JELLY--HE WAS SLIPPERY AND YOU COULDN'T GET A HOLD ON HIM.
UM ...
CHOUKO-CHAN?
...HE WAS SOMEONE WHO COULD GIVE EVERYTHING HE HAD TO PROTECT SOMEONE.
AKIYAMA-SAN.

BUT I THINK THAT THE THINGS THAT OVERFLOW FROM WANTING TO CONVEY THEM...
WANTING THEM TO REACH SOMEONE,
ARE VERY PRECIOUS.
...JUST LIKE HOW THAT GRUFF, STUBBORN, PIG-HEADED AUTHOR WHO CAN'T BE HONEST WITH HIMSELF ...
...JUST COULDN'T HELP...
WANTING TO KEEP AN ADORABLE HIGH SCHOOL GIRL WITH HIM...
AND WROTE *HANA!* YOU KNOW?
AKIYAMA-SAN...

CLINK
THANK YOU FOR YOUR HARD WORK.
OH!
THANKS!
...HOW DID THE BOOK ORGANIZATION GO?
IT WENT WELL!
HE SHOULD BE DONE IN ABOUT FIVE OR SIX YEARS.
...
How can I get him to stop...?
...
CHOUKO-CHAN.
DO YOU REMEMBER BEFORE ...
WHEN I SAID THAT...
"WORDS AREN'T THAT IMPORTANT"...?
THERE WAS A TIME WHEN I WAS COMPLETELY USELESS, AND SO WERE WORDS WITH NO SUBSTANCE.
THAT'S WHY I SAID THAT.

I DON'T WANNA.
I AM KEI...
...MIZU-SHIMA'S ...
BEST FRIEND, AFTER ALL.
...
DON'T JUST DECIDE THAT.
CHEEP
TWEET TWEET

SOB SOB
MAYBE I'LL STEAL TWO OR THREE.
SOB SOB
UGH.
WHAT IS WITH YOU?
YOU NEVER, EVER LEARN.
WHEN THE HECK WILL YOU FINALLY GET SICK OF ME?
HAVING SOMEONE LIKE YOU NEARBY MAKES ME SO SICK I CAN'T STAND IT...
WHY DON'T YOU...
...JUST WASH YOUR HANDS OF ME ALREADY?

INHALE
KEI!
SLAM!
I HEAR YOU'RE ORGANIZING YOUR BOOKS?
I'LL HELP!
WAAAH, KEI!
FWOOSH
FWOOSH
FWOOSH
はっきはっきはっき
WH--
WHAT KIND OF BOOBY TRAPS ARE IN THIS PLACE...?
HUFF
HUFF
HUFF
HUFF
I'M THE ONE WHO WAS SCARED, YOU MORON ...
DOING
DOING
BRISK
BRISK
WHAT?
ARE YOU ORGANIZING BY YEAR OR BY AUTHOR?
ZAM
ZAM
...
GYAAAAAH!
A HIDEHO CHIKU FIRST EDITION, BROKEN IN TWO!
I CAN DO WHAT I WANT. SHUT UP.

IF...
IF YOU'RE HAPPY, MIZUSHIMA-SAN.
THAT'S...
THAT'S ENOUGH!
WHAT I WANT MOST.
...
YES ...

AND AFTER ALL...
I DON'T ...
...KNOW ANYTHING ABOUT HIM.
...
AND YOU'RE STILL--
I'M ...
...HAPPY NOW.
SO HAPPY IT MAKES ME DIZZY.
I'LL ...
BE GOING ...
...

IT'S HIS FAULT...
...THAT YOU...
...SUFFERED SO MUCH.
...
YES.
I THINK...
HE'S KIND OF...
SCARY.
...
HE...
SCARES ME, TOO.

NOTHING.
THEN PLEASE LET ME THROUGH...
...AH!
SS
Kyaaa!
KARASAWA-SAN, YOU WERE AWAKE!??!
YES.
I HEARD EVERYTHING.
UM,
THAT SENSEI...
DON'T YOU THINK THERE'S KIND OF A PROBLEM WITH HIM...?
I-I WAS A L-LITTLE SURPRISED, TOO...
...ARE SURE ABOUT HIM?

Good morning!
KEI-SAN!
YOU'RE UP AWFULLY EARLY.
That's unusual.
GROG GROG
NO, I DIDN'T SLEEP.
...YOU WERE READING, WEREN'T YOU...?
Please don't make yourself sick...
BULL'S EYE
...
WHAT'S THAT?
OH...
THIS...?
WATER AND MEDICINE FOR KARASAWA-SAN.
AKIYAMA-SAN IS THE SAME AS ALWAYS,
BUT KARASAWA-SAN REALLY SEEMED TO BE SUFFERING LAST NIGHT.
PATTER PATTER
S S
?
WH--
WHAT IS IT?
...

CHOU.

DRAG

DRAG

I KNOCKED ONE OUT.

... THIS ONE ...

SELF-DESTRUCTED, TOO ...

SNORRRRE

SNORRRRE

SNORRRE

...

... SHOULD WE PUT 'EM OUTSIDE?

It won't kill 'em.

...

RIGHT ...

CHIRP

CHIRP

THE NEXT MORNING...

I READ THIS GUY'S NOVEL, YOU KNOW!??!
IT'S REALLY GREAT!
Are--
NO, IT'S REALLY NOT GREAT, BUT!
Are you all right?
No, I can't go on. I really can't.
HE WRITES DOWN THE SUBTLE CHANGES IN MENTALITY WITHOUT LETTING ANYTHING LEAK OUT.
HIS STYLE ISN'T POLISHED AT ALL, AND HIS COMPOSITION SO-SO, BUT ITS THICK PSYCHOLOGICAL DESCRIPTIONS GIVE IT A STRANGE KIND OF CHARM.
SSSSHHHH
WORDS SURE ARE INTERESTING, HUH, KEI!
OH, I SEE, I SEE. GOOD FOR YOU.
WAIT--
KEI-SA ...
I'M DYING!
HERE'S SOME WATER. DRINK ALL YOU WANT.
BURBLE BURBLE
WASH BASIN
COUGH
BLECH
... UGH.
WHAT DO YOU MEAN, "SHINICHI-SAN"?
ARE YOU STUPID?
MUTTER MUTTER
... KEI.
DON'T BE JEALOUS.

GOOD EEEEEVENING!
EVE-NING!!
AKIYAMA HERE!
KARASAWA HERE.
WELL, WE HAPPENED TO RUN INTO EACH OTHER AT JINBOUCHOU AND WENT DRINKING AT CHAMIZU AND KICHIJOUJI...
THEN WE KEPT GOING WITH THE FLOW AND ENDED UP HERE!
HERE!!
OH, COULD I GET SOME WATER!??! I BEEN TALKING SO MUCH MY THROAT HURTS!!
MAN, KARASAWA-KUN IS INCREDIBLE!! HE'S SO YOUNG, BUT THERE'S NO ONE IN ALL OF JAPAN WHO CAN KEEP UP WITH ME LIKE HE CAN!!
OH, NOT AT ALL.
I DON'T EVEN HOLD A CAMERA (HIC) TO THE DEPTH OF YOUR INTERPRETATION, SHINICHI-SAN...
CLING!
OH NOBITA! FRIEND OF MY HEART! FILL UP BALLOON.
CHOU.
SALT.
GET SOME SALT.
...
LISTEN TO THIS, KEI!!

[NOTE: IN JAPAN, SALT IS USED IN PURIFICATION AND EXORCISM RITUALS. KEI IS TELLING CHOUKO TO GET THE SALT SO HE CAN EXORCISE HIS HOUSE OF THESE NEW PESTS.]

KEI-SAN
...
...
DING-
DOOONG

UM,
I'LL...
...DO MY BEST!
SO PLEASE ASK ME ANYTHING...!
....
HMM.
THEN, TOMORROW...
LET'S GO VISIT YOUR GRANDFATHER IN THE HOSPITAL.
...TOGETHER.
I WOULD LIKE TO MEET HIM.

WINCE!
CRASH
CLINK
I WAS JUST PUTTING MY TEACUP DOWN.
Y-YES!
YOU DID JUST PUT YOUR TEACUP DOWN!!
...
I WON'T BITE YOU AGAIN. CALM DOWN.
CRASH
K--
KE--
GOOD NIGHT.
CRACK
KEI-SAN!
JERK
NN?

I DO THINK THIS VOLUME HAS AN UNUSUAL FEEL TO IT COMPARED TO THE OTHERS, BUT IT'S STILL *THE NAME OF THE FLOWER,* AND I HOPE YOU ALL ENJOY IT.

MY EDITOR.
...REALLY, THANK YOU FOR EVERYTHING....

EVERYONE WHO HELPED ME.

AMANO-SAMA,
MIKAMI-SAMA,
MORINAGA-SAMA,
KAMIJOU-SAMA,
KISARAGI-SAMA.

THANK YOU VERY MUCH.

EVERYONE WHO SENT ME LETTERS.
I TREASURE READING THEM. REALLY, THANK YOU SO MUCH!

EVERYONE WHO SUPPORTED ME, THANK YOU VERY MUCH!

IF IT'S ALRIGHT, PLEASE LET ME KNOW WHAT YOU THINK.

↓

KEN SAITO
C/O CMX
888 PROSPECT STREET
SUITE 240
LA JOLLA, CA 92037

I DON'T KNOW...
...IF HE'S REALLY CLEANING...
...OR WHAT.
TOSS
RUSTLE
TOSS
TOSS
TICK
TICK
EH !!??!
HOW DID IT GET TO BE SO LATE!??!
WHAT WERE YOU DOING?
WHAT?
KEI-SAN.
YOU'RE STILL AWAKE?
OH,
I THOUGHT I'D LEARN FROM YOUR EXAMPLE AND CLEAN AROUND THE HOUSE.
Starting in the kitchen.
LOOK AT THIS POT!!
Really excited
LOOK HOW SHINY IT IS WITH JUST A LITTLE POLISH-ING!!
... YEAH.
Amazing.

PATTER PATTER
KEI-SAN!
ARE YOU ALL RIGHT ...!??!
... YEAH.
IT WAS JUST AN AVA-LANCHE.
DON'T WORRY ABOUT IT.
....
UM,
SHOULD I...
HELP OUT...?
WINCE
SUPER BLUNT
NO.
DON'T YOU TOUCH ANY-THING.
...
A WHILE AGO...
...KEI-SAN STARTED CLEANING HIS ROOM, AS IF HE WAS POSSESSED.
HE EVEN STARTED ORGANIZING THE BOOKS IN HIS CLOSET.
RUSTLE
RUSTLE

MARI-GOLDS...
VIOLETS...
AZALEAS.
IN THE SUMMER, WE CAN HAVE...
SUN-FLOWERS.
IRISES.
GLADIOLAS...
WHAT WILL I PLANT *THIS* YEAR?
THUD THUD THUD

花の名前
The Name of the Flower
CHAPTER 15

KEI-SAN
...
THE NAME OF THE FLOWER CHAPTER 14 / END

DO...
...I NEED ...
...ANY MORE REASON THAN THAT TO BE BESIDE YOU...?

I...
...CAN'T HELP MYSELF ANYMORE.
I LOVE YOU TOO MUCH, KEI-SAN.

IT DOESN'T MATTER ...
...HOW MANY...
...TIMES YOU FALL.
I'LL ALWAYS ...
...STAY...
...BY YOUR SIDE.

I DON'T CARE.
IT'S YOUR FAULT.
IT'S BECAUSE YOU SHOW ME THOSE SCENES.
NO MATTER HOW MUCH YOU MAY REGRET IT...
I'LL NEVER LET YOU GO.

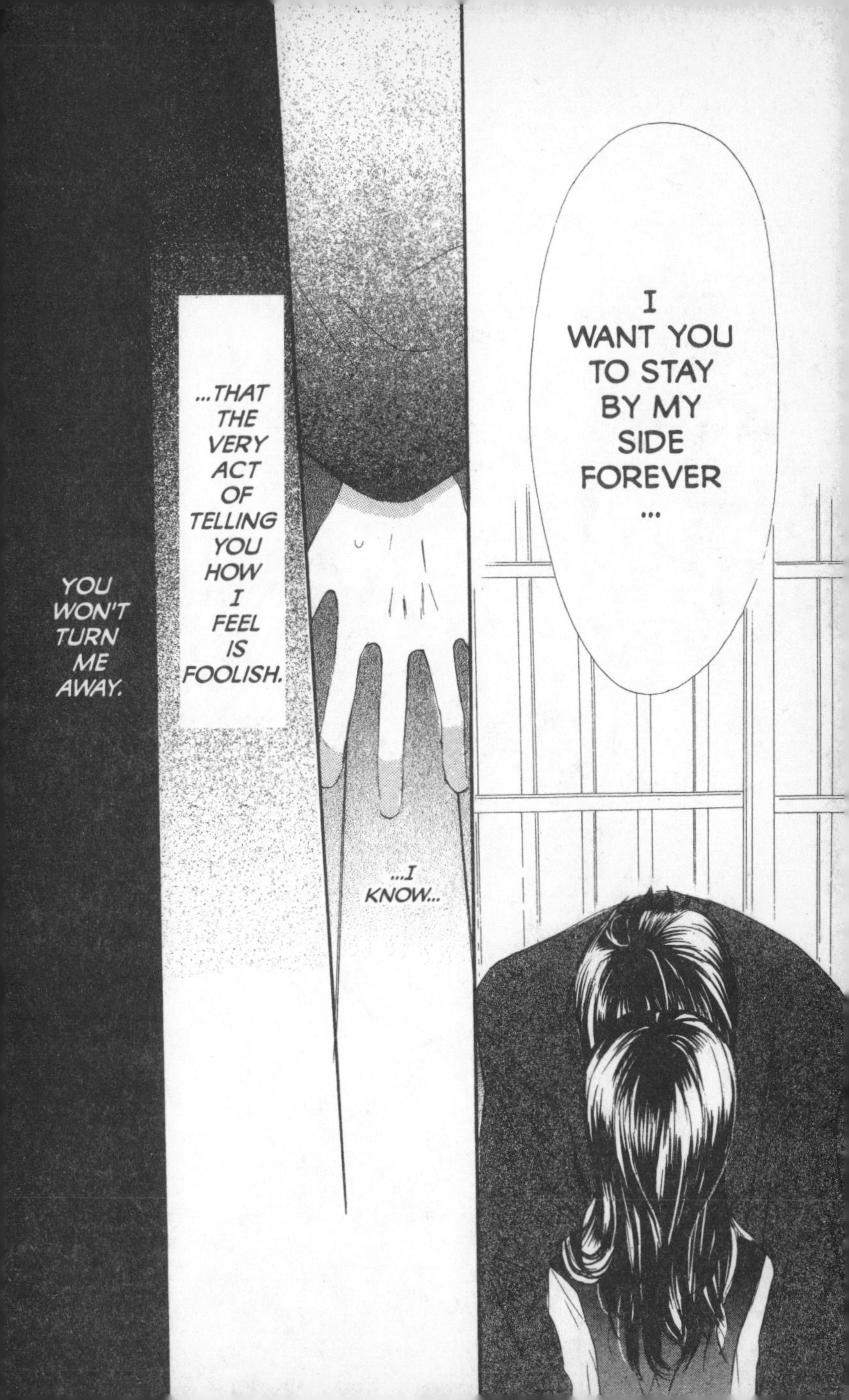

I WANT YOU TO STAY BY MY SIDE FOREVER...

...I KNOW...

...THAT THE VERY ACT OF TELLING YOU HOW I FEEL IS FOOLISH.

YOU WON'T TURN ME AWAY.

I WAS AFRAID THAT IF I...
...CLUNG TO YOU...
I WOULD DRAG YOU INTO IT.
I WAS RUNNING AWAY...
BUT...
...NOW...
I DON'T ...
...WANT TO LOSE YOU.
EVER.

AH ...
PLOP
I'M A...
...HOPELESS HUMAN BEING.
I KEEP...
...GETTING CAUGHT IN THE SAME...
...DARKNESS OVER AND OVER AGAIN.
I FALL...
...AND IT ALL HAPPENS AGAIN.

RATTLE
RATTLE
CHOU.
SIT DOWN.
EH?

I DON'T HAVE ANY RIGHT TO HAVE YOU CARE ABOUT ME, SHIN-KUN.
I'M SORRY...
FOR LETTING YOU RUN AWAY...

...
YEAH.
I...
...GOT YOU INVOLVED BECAUSE I KNEW HOW YOU FELT...
SHIN-KUN.
I DIDN'T WANT...
...THERE TO BE ANYTHING LEFT FOR HIM AFTER I WAS GONE.
I KNOW ...

IT'S NOT FAIR.
HE DRAGGED ME INTO IT, AND NOW I CAN'T GET OUT OF IT EITHER.
SO WHY IS *HE* THE ONLY ONE...
...TO FALL IN LOVE?
BUT
HE FINALLY...
...RAISED HIS HEAD AND LOOKED AT ME...
...AND THAT'S ENOUGH.

IT...
SURPRISED ME WHEN I READ IT.
TO THINK THAT KEI WOULD LOOK AT SOMEONE SO WARMLY.
IT MADE ME WONDER HOW...
HE WOULD LOOK AT *ME*, AFTER WRITING A STORY LIKE THAT.
BECAUSE NOTHING EVER CHANGES.
I ...
ABANDONED EVERYTHING.
NO MATTER HOW MUCH I DROVE KEI INTO A CORNER THE WAY HE WANTS...
HE NEVER ONCE TRIED TO LOOK AT ME.
HE AVERTED HIS EYES LIKE HE ALWAYS DID.
IT MADE ME ANGRY.

SHIN-KUN.
YOU WERE WATCHING?
NO.
I *KNOW* YOU,
IORI.
BECAUSE YOU WALKED LIKE A BRILLIANT LIGHT AHEAD OF ME...
...LIKE AN IDIOT...
I ALWAYS, ALWAYS...
FOLLOWED YOU.
HANA ...

NO.
I...
...HAVE WORK.
I NEED TO GET BACK.
GOODBYE.

SQUEEEZE...
...?

...
...?
I THINK YOU DROPPED IT WHEN WE BUMPED INTO EACH OTHER IN THE RAIN.
... YES.
...IT REALLY IS...
THIS IS YOURS, ISN'T IT?
EH?
OH!
YOU DIDN'T NEED TO COME ALL THIS WAY...
Thank you very much.
UH,
UM.
IF IT'S ALL RIGHT, I CAN TREAT YOU TO TEA AS THANKS...

WHOOOOSH
......
THE SUNSET IS BEAUTI-FUL...
ISN'T IT...?

WHY...
DO YOU...
THINK I ...
...WAS ABLE TO USE THESE HANDS TO SWEEP THE DARKNESS AWAY?
...
YOU'RE STRONG.
IT'S BECAUSE I HAD YOU.

PLEASE...
LET GO OF MY HAND.
...
ALL-RIGHT.
......
TOUCHING SOMEONE LIKE ME...
YOUR PRECIOUS HANDS...
THE HANDS THAT SWEPT AWAY YOUR DARKNESS...
WILL GET DIRTY.
SQUEEZE
...
AND WHY...?

...
ARE YOU ...
...AWAKE?
...
...WHAT?
WHERE ...?
THE PARK NEAR THE HOUSE.
I TOLD YOU I WAS GOING OUT SHOPPING, AND YOU INSISTED ON COMING WITH ME, SO WE CAME OUTSIDE. BUT YOU STOPPED FEELING WELL ON THE WAY THERE, SO WE WERE RESTING.
DON'T YOU REMEMBER...?
SO YOU REALLY **WERE** DELIRIOUS ...
I did think it was strange.
I'M SORRY.
DAZE
DAZE
I'm going with you.
But Kei-san, you're not well...
O-of course not...
No, I'm going. You gonna leave me here?
You kept insisting, so...
...

I HAVE TO PAY FOR WHAT I DID ...
...UNDER THIS EMPTY SKY.

...WAS MY FAULT.
... KEI-KUN.
LOOK ...
SEE?
WHAT A BEAUTIFUL SUNSET.

...I THOUGHT THAT, TOO.
SNIP
THAT...
I WOULD ALWAYS PROTECT HER.
SNIP
...
YOUR MOTHER?
I SAID SOME-THING TERRIBLE AND HURT HER.
SHE WAS STILL HURT ...
WHEN SHE DIED.
SNIP
ALL OF IT-- EVERYTHING ...
...
OH.
SNIP
IT WAS HARD, WASN'T IT?
NOT BEING ABLE TO SAY YOU'RE SORRY.
......
SNIP
EVEN IF I DID APOLOGIZE...
...SHE WOULD NEVER...
SNIP
...FORGIVE ME.

SNIP
SNIP
WHAT DO YOU LIKE SO MUCH ABOUT THAT GUY?
SOMEONE LIKE YOU...
...COULD CHOOSE LOTS OF OTHER GUYS, RIGHT?
I CAN'T.
HARU-KUN IS AN IDIOT.
SO I DECIDED I WOULD TAKE CARE OF HIM FOR THE REST OF MY LIFE.
...

...TOLD ME THAT IT'S MORE IMPORTANT FOR HIM TO STAY WITH YOU THAN TO...
...PURSUE THE BOTANICAL RESEARCH HE LOVES MORE THAN LIFE ITSELF.
HE SAYS YOU'RE SO CUTE, AND HE FEELS SO BAD FOR YOU, THAT HE CAN'T LEAVE YOU ALONE.
BLUSH
IT'S NOT LIKE I ASKED HIM TO...!
I KNOW.
I'M TAKING HIM BACK.
I'M SORRY.
THAT HARU-KUN.
AS LONG AS YOU'RE WALKING UNSTEADILY LIKE THAT...
I'M SURE HE WOULD STAY WITH YOU FOREVER.
BUT YOU KNOW THAT'S NOT GOOD FOR YOU.
...
I'M GOING TO CUT YOUR HAIR.
COME OVER HERE, KEI-KUN.

DON'T YOU...
...THINK YOUR BANGS ARE TOO LONG?
YOU CAN'T SEE WITH THEM LIKE THAT.
BRUSH
WINCE
SHOULD I CUT THEM FOR YOU?
...
HARU-KUN...

This man...
SLURRRP SLURRRP
WHERE'S CHOU-CHAN? DID YOU LEAVE HER AT HOME?
OF COURSE NOT!! I LEFT HER WITH MY DAD!
NGH...!
Erk!
ARE YOU SERIOUS? HE'S GONNA YELL AT ME AGAIN.
DON'T WORRY. HE WAS *REALLY* EXASPERATED.
...
...
I DON'T LIKE IT...
RATTLE RATTLE
WELCOME BACK, KEI-KUN.
...
WHERE'S COUSIN YOH...?
HE WENT TO APOLOGIZE TO THE PROFESSOR.
BUT THE PROFESSOR MOST LIKELY WON'T LISTEN TO HIM.
...HE'LL PROBABLY BE BACK LATE.
...
KEI-KUN.

MAN, SORRY FOR ALL THE FUSS!
MY WIFE HAS CALMED DOWN CONSID-ERABLY!
... YOUR WIFE?
YUP.
SAKURA MIZUSHIMA-CHAN.
HARU-KUN TOLD ME EVERYTHING.
YOU MUST HAVE BEEN THROUGH A LOT.
SORRY FOR BEING SO UPSET EARLIER.
I was angry.
RUSTLE
AS AN APOLOGY, I'LL MAKE DINNER FOR YOU!
MY COOKING IS ON A COMPLETELY DIFFERENT LEVEL FROM WHATEVER HARU-KUN THROWS TOGETHER.
LOOK FOR-WARD TO IT!
MINE IS A MAN'S COOK-ING!
WHAT?! WHO DO YOU THINK TAUGHT YOU HOW TO COOK?
HARU-KUN?
SHE'S AN IDIOT, SO SHE THINKS THAT MY NAME IS READ "HARUKA."
WHO ARE YOU CALLING AN IDIOT?
PIIINCH
[EDITOR'S NOTE: THE CHINESE SYMBOL FOR "YOH" CAN ALSO BE READ "HARUKA."]

YOU SAID THAT YOU WANTED TO DO WHATEVER IT TOOK TO GET INTO A LABORATORY,
SO I THOUGHT YOU WERE STUDYING HARD, HARU-KUN!
AND I EVEN DEALT WITH BEING AWAY FROM Y-- MMPH!
KEI,
I'M SORRY.
JINGLE
YOU GO ON HOME.
Let go of me, stupid!
...
CAW CAW
DING-DOOONG
RATTLE RATTLE
THE NAME OF THE FLOWER 3-PANEL COMIC
~ONE DAY~
1
YOU REALLY ARE GOOD AT ALL KINDS OF GAMES, AKIYAMA-SAN.
Ha ha ha.
Go
WELL, I LIKE THEM.
2
YUP!
SNAP
ARE YOU BETTER THAN KEI-SAN?
3
ONE TIME, KEI FLIPPED OVER THE SHOGI BOARD ON ME!
Come to think of it, we haven't played once since then.
SNAP
FIN

KAPOW!
YOU ...
STUPID JERK!!!
I CALLED PROFESSOR OHKOUCHI AND HEARD YOU WERE FIRED!
HE WAS FURIOUS!
SHRILL
HE SAID YOU HADN'T BEEN TO THE SCHOOL IN A WHOLE MONTH!!
S-- SAKURA-CHAN ...
NO ...
JUST LET ...
SHRILL
LISTEN TO ME...
I CAN'T GET A HOLD OF YOU, YOU WERE KICKED OUT OF YOUR APARTMENT--WHAT HAVE YOU BEEN DOING, YOU IDIOT!?!

UNTIL I LOST IT.
TED TED
TED TED
... SAKURA-CHAN ...

HE JUST...
STAYED BESIDE ME.
AT THE TIME...
EVERYTHING THAT SURROUNDED ME WEIGHED ON ME LIKE LEAD.
HAVING SOME-ONE NEXT TO ME...
SEEING THE SAME THINGS ...
I WOULDN'T KNOW HOW HEALING IT WAS.
OR HOW MUCH...
...I NEEDED IT.

FROM THAT DAY...
YOH ...
...DID EVERYTHING WITH ME, FROM MORNING UNTIL NIGHT.
I SAID NOTHING TO HIM.
AND HE...
ASKED NOTHING.

HE JUST...

SHOVE
...
I DON'T KNOW WHAT HAPPENED.
BUT HOW WOULD KILLING YOU WHEN YOU *WANT* TO DIE BE A PUNISHMENT?
IF YOU WANT TO PAY FOR SOMETHING YOU'VE DONE...
WHEN HE SAID IT...
THEN LIVE...
AND ENDURE IT ...
COUSIN YOH...
COVERED MY EYES FOR SOME REASON.

...
DON'T STOP ME.
LET ME DIE...
DON'T BE STUPID, KEI.
THEN...
...KILL ME, PLEASE!
COUSIN YOH...!!
WHAM!
PLEASE.
GIVE ME MY PUNISHMENT ...!

I DIDN'T EVEN KNOW HOW MUCH TIME WAS MISSING FROM MY MEMORIES.
CRASH!
KEI?
STUPID ...!
ガッ
GRAB!
WHAT ARE YOU DOING?

CHAPTER 14

AFTER IORI SHOWED UP, MY EDITOR'S *AORI* (THE BLURB WRITTEN ON THE TITLE PAGE WHEN THE COMIC IS IN THE MAGAZINE) GOT REALLY SERIOUS. EVERY TIME, MY HEART WOULD POUND AS I LOOKED AT IT, WONDERING HOW FAR THEY'RE GOING TO GO, SO I THINK I'LL PRESENT SOME OF THEM HERE.

CHAPTER 10: "LOST IN THE LUSTER OF FALLING PETALS..." CHAPTER 11: "THE FLOWER OF MADNESS THAT BLOOMS IN THE SETTING SUN'S LIGHT..." CHAPTER 12: "CHERRY BLOSSOMS OF INSANITY..."

WHEN IT WENT AS FAR AS "CHERRY BLOSSOMS OF INSANITY," I CALLED AND ASKED, "CHERRY BLOSSOMS OF INSANITY?" AND MY EDITOR SAID, "YUP. KUBOZUKA!" IT'S A SECRET THAT I WAS STRUCK SPEECHLESS AT THE RECEIVER. [NOTE: YOSUKE KUBOZUKA IS AN ACTOR WHO WAS IN A MOVIE CALLED *KYOUKI NO SAKURA,* WHICH CAN TRANSLATE TO CHERRY BLOSSOMS OF INSANITY.]

OH, I SEE...
IT'S LIKE COUSIN YOH ...
AFTER MY MOTHER DIED...
I WOKE UP IN THE HOSPITAL.

I'LL BE HERE THE NEXT TIME...
...YOU OPEN YOUR EYES, TOO.
SO, PLEASE...
GET PLENTY OF REST.
WHAT...
......
...IS THIS...
...SENSE OF DÉJÁ VU?

I DON'T WANT ANY.
KEI-SA ...
BRUSH
WINCE
...I SAID TERRIBLE THINGS TO YOU.
WHY ARE YOU STILL THERE...?
... HMM.
I DON'T KNOW ...
BUT ...

...N.
KEI-SAN.
ARE YOU ALRIGHT?
......
CHOU ...
WHAT ...?
YOU HAD A FEVER AND PASSED OUT.
YOU'VE BEEN HAVING NIGHT-MARES SINCE LAST NIGHT...
DO YOU...
THINK YOU CAN EAT SOME-THING?
I'M NOT HUNGRY.
BUT KEI-SAN...
YOU NEED MEDICINE.
NO.

AS THE CHERRY BLOSSOM PETALS SCATTERED IN A FRENZY AROUND ME...
SHE'S HOPELESS.
HOW MANY TIMES DID I TELL HER TO TAKE CARE OF HERSELF...?
...MY THOUGHTS WHIRLED...
SHE'S A ... WEAK ... FRAIL PERSON ...
I HAVE TO PROTECT HER...
AROUND AND AROUND ...
AND JUST STOPPED.

THE NEXT MORNING...
...WHEN I WENT DOWN THE STAIRS...
...MY MOTHER WAS DEAD.
I FOUND OUT...
SHE HADN'T TAKEN...
THE MEDI-CINE ...
THAT WAS RIGHT THERE...
NEXT TO HER.

WHAP
DON'T TOUCH ME!
YOU'RE FILTHY...!
I'LL NEVER FORGET...
...THE LOOK ON HER FACE.

IS IT...
TRUE...
...THAT I WAS BORN BECAUSE YOU HAD AN AFFAIR WITH GRANDFA-THER...?
...
SAY IT'S NOT TRUE...
TWITCH
...KEI.
LET'S JUST TAKE CARE OF YOUR HAND.

CLATTER
KEI!
WHERE WERE YOU?
I WAS WORRI--
WHAT HAP-PENED?
YOUR HAND--IT'S HURT...
SSSH
...
I SAW...
MY BROTHER.
HE TOLD ME
WHY...
YOU GOT DIVORCED.
......
IS IT TRUE?
MOM.

SHE'S DOING WORSE THAN BEFORE
IF I COULD JUST TALK TO HER DOCTOR--TO MIFUNE-SAN--
WHAT GUTTER THAT WOMAN DIES IN HAS NOTHING TO DO WITH ME.
OH...
YEAH.
YOU DON'T KNOW.
LET ME TELL YOU...
GRIND.
WHY YOU ...
AND THAT WOMAN WERE DRIVEN OUT OF THIS HOUSE.
HH...

WHAT ARE YOU DOING?
DON'T CROSS THE GATE INTO MY HOUSE WITH THOSE FILTHY FEET.
... SEI ...
S-- SEI-SAMA!
WHAT ARE YOU ...
AYA.
WHAT FAMILY DO YOU SERVE?
DON'T BOTHER WITH SOMEONE WHO HAS NOTHING TO DO WITH THE KATAOKAS.
SPLASH
...!
IT'S MOM!

SSSSHHH...
KEI-SAMA!
...
... AYA-SAN.
OH, GOOD I--
WHAT'S THE MATTER?
WHY ARE YOU OUT IN THE RAIN ...!??!
NEVER MIND THAT.
WILL YOU TAKE A MESSAGE TO MIFUNE-SAN?
WHACK!
SPLASH!
MY MOTHER'S ...
ERK!

...AND SET OUT IN THE RAIN FOR THE KATAOKA HOUSE.

THE PILLS TO STOP HER ATTACKS.
THE FAMILY DOCTOR AT THE KATAOKA HOUSE USED TO MAKE THEM FOR HER...
HOW LONG WILL THESE LAST?
MY FRAIL, FRAGILE MOTHER.
IF NO ONE PROTECTS HER, SHE'LL DIE.
...I WAS SWALLOWED UP BY ANXIETY AND IMPATIENCE.
I TOOK ALL OUR SAVINGS...

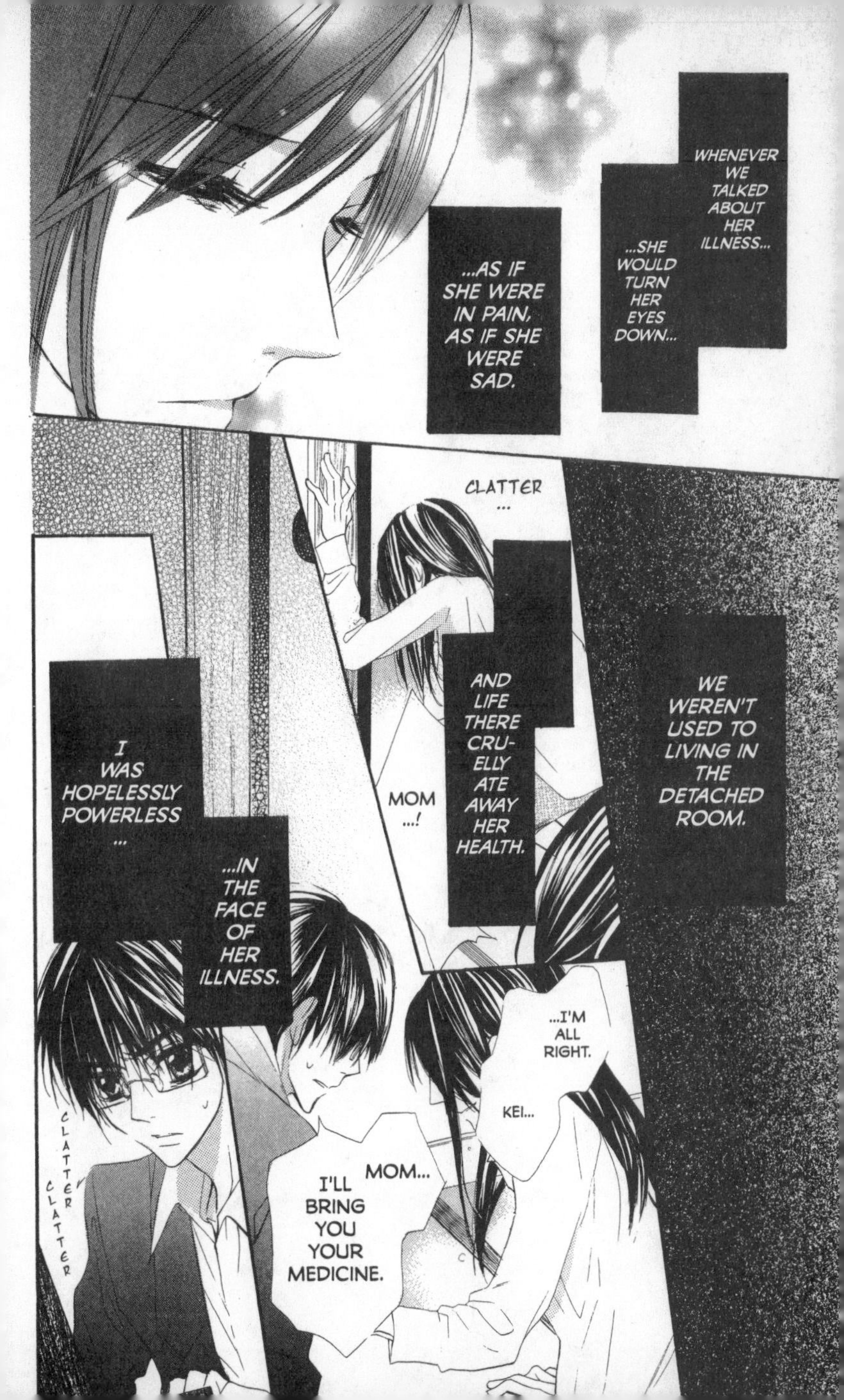
WHENEVER WE TALKED ABOUT HER ILLNESS...
...SHE WOULD TURN HER EYES DOWN...
...AS IF SHE WERE IN PAIN, AS IF SHE WERE SAD.
WE WEREN'T USED TO LIVING IN THE DETACHED ROOM.
AND LIFE THERE CRU-ELLY ATE AWAY HER HEALTH.
CLATTER ...
MOM ...!
I WAS HOPELESSLY POWERLESS ...
...IN THE FACE OF HER ILLNESS.
...I'M ALL RIGHT.
KEI...
MOM...
I'LL BRING YOU YOUR MEDICINE.
CLATTER
CLATTER

MOM!
... YOU'RE GOING TO WORK?
CLATTER
YES.
... YOU CAN'T.
WHAT IF YOU HAVE AN ATTACK?
...
I'LL WORK AS SOON AS I'M DONE WITH MIDDLE SCHOOL...
UNTIL THEN, IT DOESN'T MATTER WHAT THEY SAY ABOUT US.
WE'LL JUST LET THE MIZUSHIMAS TAKE CARE OF US.
MOM,
YOU JUST THINK ABOUT YOUR HEALTH FIRST.
TAKE YOUR MEDICINE AND RECUPERATE.
... KEI.
MY MOTHER WAS BORN WITH A WEAK HEART.

WHAP!
DON'T TOUCH ME...
RIGHT, RIGHT,
BEG-GING YOUR PARDON ♡
I DESPISED MY FRIVOLOUS COUSIN.
EW, THAT'S CREEPY ...!!!
...KEI.
YOH-SAN...
...COMES TO SEE US BECAUSE HE'S WORRIED ABOUT US.
YOU SHOULD AT LEAST GIVE HIM A PROPER HELLO.
...
EVEN TODAY. HE WAS HERE TO TELL ME ABOUT A JOB OFFER.

OH, KEI!
HI!
WELCOME BACK!
KEI!
Ignoring me !??!
YOH MIZUSHIMA WAS MY MOTHER'S NEPHEW...
...AND I HEARD THAT HE WAS AN ASSISTANT PROFESSOR AT A COLLEGE IN KYOTO.
APPARENTLY HE HAD ABANDONED THE FIANCÉE THEIR FAMILIES HAD BETROTHED HIM TO, ELOPED, AND BEEN DISOWNED FROM THE MIZUSHIMA FAMILY.
KEI!
DID HE THINK HE AND MY MOTHER WERE IN A SIMILAR SITUATION?
HE WOULD SHOW UP IN OUR ROOM WHEN THE MIZUSHIMA FAMILY WASN'T LOOKING.
...WHAT DO YOU WANT?
Ha ha.
DON'T BE SO HARSH.
I HAD TO TAKE THIS JOB AND LEAVE MY SUPER CUTE WIFE AND DAUGHTER IN TOKYO, YOU KNOW? AT LEAST GIVE ME A SIGHT FOR SORE EYES!
COME ON!
PAT

WHEN THEIR DAUGHTER CAME BACK AFTER A FAILED POLITICAL MARRIAGE...
...THEY DIDN'T HIDE THEIR DISDAIN FOR HER.
PEDIGREE AND SOCIAL STATUS...
WERE MORE IMPORTANT THAN ANYTHING TO MY MOTHER'S FAMILY.
MIZUSHIMA
MY MOTHER AND I WERE SHUNTED INTO A DETACHED ROOM THAT WAS PRACTICALLY A SHACK.
IN THIS INFERIOR ENVIRONMENT, I RESOLVED...
...THAT I WOULD PROTECT MY FRAIL MOTHER.
RATTLE RATTLE
Ha ha ha
...OH, STOP IT, YOH-SAN.
NO, REALLY!
THERE'S NO ONE AS PRETTY AS YOU, NAGISA-SAN.
AND WHEN I SAY IT, THERE'S NO DOUBT ABOUT IT!
I'M HOME... MOM.

...STARTED ABUSING MY MOTHER.

THE MORE I TRIED TO STOP HIM...

...THE MORE PERSISTENTLY HE CONDEMNED HER.

ONE YEAR LATER...
THEY GOT A DIVORCE.
WHEN IT WAS DECIDED THAT MY MOTHER AND I WOULD LEAVE THE HOUSE...
I WAS RELIEVED WITH ALL MY HEART.

...I DIDN'T NEED TO WORRY ANYMORE...

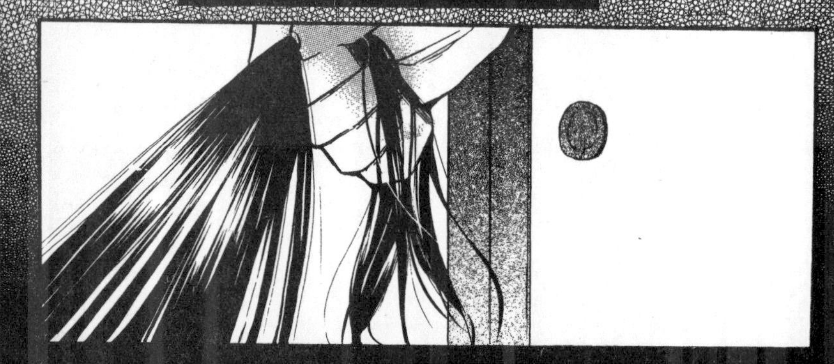

...ABOUT WHEN MY MOTHER WOULD BE BULLIED TO DEATH.

IS IT RAINING...?

THE KATAOKA HOUSEHOLD WHERE I WAS BORN AND RAISED...

...WAS A HOUSE OF RICH UPSTARTS WHO SPRANG INTO A ZAIBATSU OVERNIGHT...
...AFTER THE HUGE SUCCESS OF MY GRANDFATHER'S BUSINESS.
[EDITOR'S NOTE: ZAIBATSU = WEALTHY JAPANESE CONGLOMERATE]

IT WAS LIKE A LUXURIOUS CAGE.

WHEN I TURNED TWELVE...
MY ENTREPRENEUR GRANDFATHER DIED...
MY FATHER WAS LIKE A MACHINE, AND MY OLDER BROTHER WAS A MINIATURE VERSION OF HIM.
AND MY FATHER...
MY MOTHER...
AND I LIVED LIKE WE WERE HOLDING OUR BREATHS.

DRIP...
......
IT'S COLD.

MID-VOLUME BONUS MANGA ~PART TWO~

花の名前
はな な まえ
The Name of the Flower
CHAPTER 14

MID-VOLUME BONUS MANGA ~PART ONE~

...
KEI-SAN.
GASP
YOU HAVE A FEVER.

I DON'T ...
...WANT ANY OF IT.

THE NAME OF THE FLOWER CHAPTER 13 / END

HEH.
SALVATION.
......!
I DON'T ...

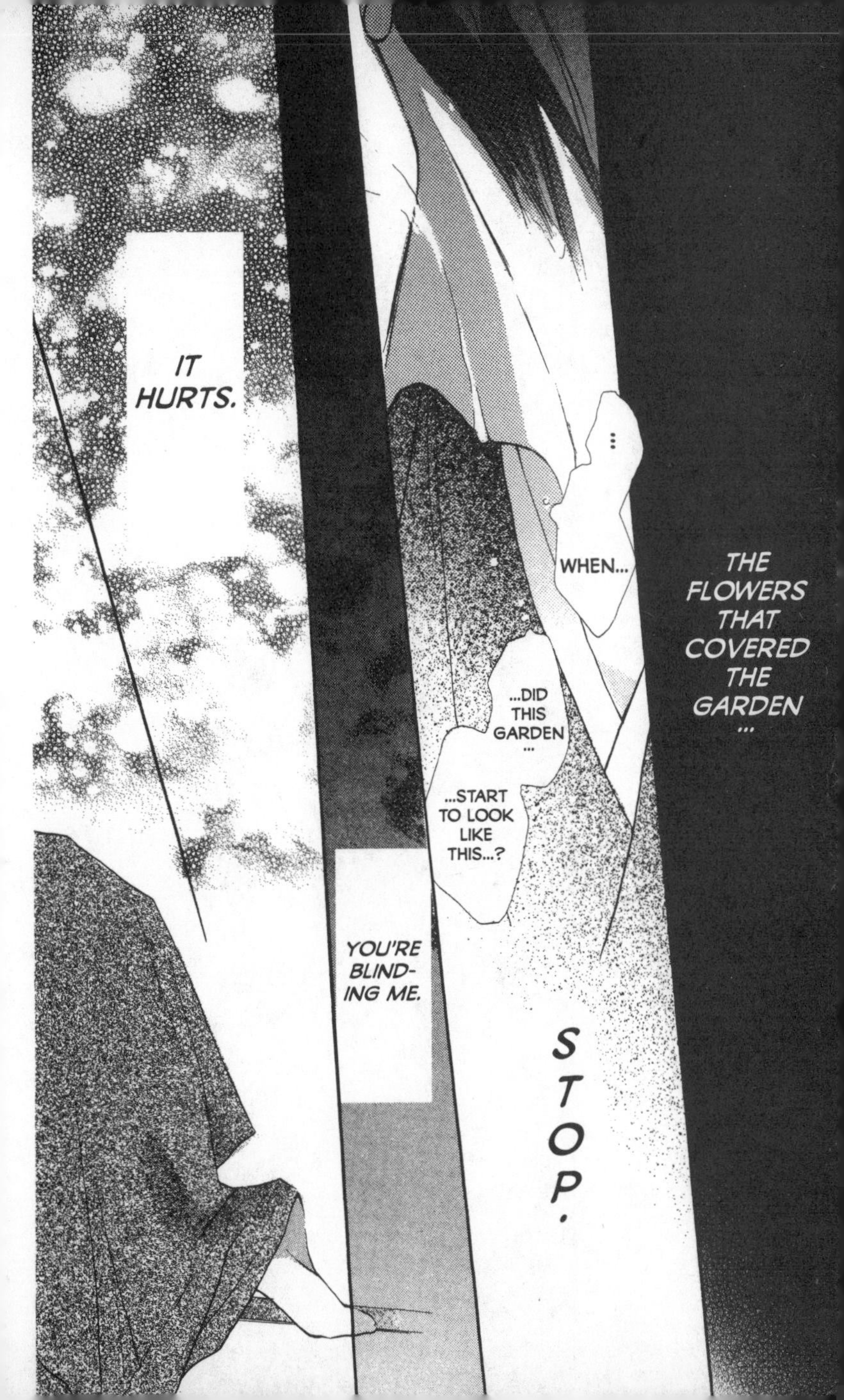

THE FLOWERS THAT COVERED THE GARDEN...
...
WHEN...
...DID THIS GARDEN...
...START TO LOOK LIKE THIS...?
STOP.
IT HURTS.
YOU'RE BLINDING ME.

... THE FLOWERS...

NO.
I...
...WON'T EVER FORGET IT HAPPENED.
I CAN'T.

...
CHOUKO-*SAN.*
WILL YOU...
...FORGET THAT YOU EVER SPENT ANY TIME WITH ME...?
I THINK YOU'RE GETTING THE WRONG IDEA ABOUT SOMETHING.
SSSSHHH...
THE ONLY REASON I TOOK YOU IN IS THAT YOU WERE SO PITIFUL IT CAPTURED MY INTEREST.
THAT'S ALL.
BUT THAT'S GONE NOW, TOO.
I'VE HAD ENOUGH...
...DO ME A FAVOR, AND GET **OUT**...

KEI-SAN
...
STOP--
TH--
WHAM
THAT HURTS...!
...
HEH
...
HA
HA!

YOU ...
...REALLY ARE SO BEAUTI-FUL.
IT'S LIKE YOU'RE MOCKING ME.
...KEI-SA--
AH.
K--
KEI-SAN!

SSSHHH
... WELCOME HOME.
I'LL BRING YOU A TOWEL.
CREAK
CREAK
... KEI-SAN.
CHILL
...... HEY.
YOU'RE NOT BROKEN ANYWHERE.

SSSSHHHH
......

WHATEVER FEELINGS ...
I MAY HAVE...
I'LL SWALLOW THEM.
FIND HAPPINESS ...
I WON'T RUN AWAY.
IORI.
PLEASE.
I'M BEGGING YOU.

...COULD REACH YOU, COULD TOUCH YOU.
I WAS A MESS OF JEALOUSY AND ENVY, HATRED, FEELING LIKE AN OUTSIDER.
I HATED YOU.
I WAS MORTIFIED.
I DESPISED YOU.
I WANTED TO KILL YOU.
YOU AND KEI.
BUT ...
...THE ONE I HATE THE MOST...
...IS **MYSELF**, FOR NOT BEING ABLE TO DO ANYTHING BUT **RUN AWAY**.
I DON'T WANT TO FEEL THAT WAY EVER AGAIN.

GIVE IT A REST.
BUT YOU ...
...RAN AWAY.
YEAH, I DID.
I COULDN'T TAKE IT.
YOU WERE BOTH FALLING SO DAMN FAR ABOVE ME, I COULDN'T REACH.
NOT A SINGLE WORD I SAID...

...
ARE YOU STUPID?
GIVE ME THAT...
I'LL GIVE IT BACK TO HER.
YOU DON'T GET IT...
SHIN-KUN.
WITHOUT ME...
KEI--

SSSHHH...
POM
I'M IMPRESSED ...
SHIN-KUN.
IORI.
HOW DID YOU GET KEI OUT?
...
OH.
LOOK.
I PICKED IT UP EARLIER.
CHOUKO-CHAN'S PASS CASE.
SHE'LL BE IN TROUBLE IF SHE DOESN'T GET IT BACK.

YES.
SSSSHHH
BAM
KYA!
SPLASH
AH!
I-I'M SORRY.
SHF..
THANK YOU VERY MUCH.
...
NOT AT ALL.
SSSHHHH...

YOU REALLY HAVE WORKED HARD ...
...
YES.
IT LOOKS LIKE IT MIGHT RAIN.
SHALL I BRING YOU AN UMBRELLA !??!
OH, THAT'S ALL-RIGHT.
...
PLEASE KEEP COMING TO SEE HIM OFTEN.
HAJIME-SENSEI
WAS ALWAYS...
...WAITING FOR YOU.

HAVE A SEAT... ...CHOUKO.
CLACK
CHOUKO.
I'M GLAD YOU CAME.
I'M THE ONE WHO SHOULD APOLOGIZE.
I'M SORRY I COULDN'T PROTECT YOU WHEN YOU NEEDED ME.
...
YOU MUST HAVE BEEN SO SAD.

I'LL GET SOME TEA.
SIT, SIT!
...
I DIDN'T KNOW WHAT I WOULD DO...
...IF I SAW YOU...
...AND LOST YOU AGAIN.
I WAS SCARED.
I WAS SO SCARED, I NEVER...
I...
I'M SORRY.

SH--
SHIMA-SAN
...I-IT'S BEEN A LONG TIME...
MY! MY... MY...
OH, DEAR! YOU SHOULD HAVE CALLED TO LET ME KNOW YOU WERE COMING!
YOU TOOK ME BY SURPRISE!
RATTLE...
NOW GO ON IN!
AH ...
HAJIME-SENSEI WILL BE SO PLEASED!
SENSEI!
SENSEI!
CHOUKO-CHAN IS HERE TO SEE YOU!
...
CHOUKO?

RATTLE RATTLE
...
603
TANIZAKI
...
WINCE
...
CHOUKO-CHAN?

WHAM!
DON'T DISAPPOINT ME...!

SHE'S STILL AT THE HOUSE...
WAITING FOR YOU.
SO STAND UP ON YOUR OWN TWO FEET AND GO HOME.
WHATEVER MAY COME OF IT...
NO MATTER...
WHAT HAPPENS TO YOU...
I'LL STAY AND SEE IT THROUGH TO THE END.
THAT GIRL ISN'T AS STRONG AS YOU THINK SHE IS.
KEI ...

RATTLE
KEI.
I KNOW YOU'RE IN THERE.
CHOUKO-CHAN...
...BROKE DOWN...
...BECAUSE OF YOU.

......
THAT'S MUSHY ...
SH-
SHUT UP!
CLICK
CRRREAK
CREAK

I ...
...DON'T THINK THAT TELLING SOMEONE YOU LIKE THEM AND HAVING THEM REJECT YOU MEANS IT'S ALL OVER.
I MEAN, IT'S NOT LIKE YOU'RE NEVER GOING TO SEE HER AGAIN...
AND NO ONE KNOWS WHAT'S GOING TO HAPPEN IN THE FUTURE.
SO, HEY.
WHY NOT JUST THINK AS HARD AS YOU CAN ABOUT WHAT YOU CAN DO FOR CHOUKO-CHAN AND WHAT YOU WANT TO DO.
IT DOESN'T MATTER WHAT...
BUT FLAILING ABOUT, WANTING TO DO SOME-THING FOR HER...
...IS NOT THE END OF THE WORLD.
WHETHER ANYTHING COMES OF IT OR NOT--THAT'S WHAT LOVE IS, ISN'T IT?
...

NO WAY!
SHE ACCEPTED !??!
NO,
SHE DUMPED ME.
SHE SAID THERE'S SOMEONE ELSE SHE LIKES.
IT'S JUST ...
I TOLD HER IN THE HEAT OF THE MOMENT.
AND AFTER I SAID IT...
...I REALIZED THAT I REALLY HAVE LIKED HER FOR A LONG, LONG TIME...
AND THE WAY I TOLD HER..
IT WAS LIKE I WAS TAKING ADVANTAGE OF HER IN HER TIME OF WEAKNESS.
I FEEL SO COMPLETELY PATHETIC.
CREAK
...
PAA-SUKE.

I FINALLY STARTED TO FEEL LIKE I WAS IN TROUBLE FROM BEING SHUT UP AT HOME FOR SO LONG, AND WITH SOME REASON LIKE, "I'LL STIMULATE MY PARASYMPATHETIC NERVES BY EATING AND INCREASE MY INSPIRATION!" THAT STOPS MAKING SENSE HALFWAY THROUGH. I INVITED MORE FRIENDS THAN EVER BEFORE TO GO OUT TO EAT. WHEN I ASKED MY READER FRIENDS WHO I HADN'T SEEN IN A LONG TIME, "WHAT DO YOU THINK OF THE MANGA I'VE BEEN DRAWING THESE DAYS?" THEY COMMENTED, "YOU'RE JUST AS GOOD AT DRAWING UNREALISTIC GIRLS AS EVER." WHEN I GOT DEPRESSED AND SAID, "I SHOULDN'T HAVE ASKED," THEY YELLED AT ME, "THAT'S A COMPLIMENT!"

GYA!
A HOUSE SPIRIT!!
Scary!
CLATTER CLATTER
WH- WHAT IS IT, PAA-SUKE?
DID YOU STAY THE NIGHT HERE?
...
...I DON'T
...HAVE ANY-WHERE TO CRY AT HOME...
RATTLE RATTLE
SIGH...
DID SOME-THING HAPPEN?
......
I TOLD...
MIZUSHIMA-SAN...
THAT I LIKE HER.
AND YOU'RE CRYING 'CAUSE SHE DUMPED YOU?
...NO.
You're such a girl!

CHIRP CHIRP
CHIRP CHIRP
RATTLE RATTLE
GOOOOOD MORNING!
CLICK
HEY, NO ONE'S GONNA BE HERE THIS EARLY.
I'm talking to myself because I hate my first class.

CHIRP
CHIRP
TWEET TWEET
CHEEEP

FELL IN LOVE.
BECAUSE I...
...CARED FOR YOU...

I LOVED IT WHEN KEI-SAN WOULD SIT ON THE VERANDA AND HIS EYES WOULD LIGHT UP A LITTLE.
HIS EYES SEEMED TO SOFTEN WHEN THEY LOOKED AT ME.
I'VE TOLD MYSELF SO MANY TIMES THAT ...
I ONLY THINK THAT BECAUSE ...
I WANT IT TO BE TRUE.

MY HEART HURTS...

I CAN'T HELP BUT...

CHASING AFTER HIM.

THE SOLITUDE MELTED INSIDE THE PAIN...

AND I STARTED TO FEAR THE DARKNESS.

BECAUSE I...

I PRAY...
...WHEN I'M GONE...
...THAT YOU WILL REMEMBER ME.

I BREATHED IN THE TIME WE SPENT TOGETHER,
SPRING,
AND THE FLOWERS...
SUMMER,
...KEPT...
FALL AND WINTER,
...INCREASING IN NUMBERS.
IN THIS GARDEN...

FEELINGS SPROUTED INSIDE ME.
...AND I WAS AFRAID TO PUT A NAME TO THEM...
BECAUSE I KNEW THEY WOULD NEVER REACH HIM.
WE HAD AGREED FROM THE START...
...THAT I WOULD LEAVE AS SOON AS I GRADUATED HIGH SCHOOL.

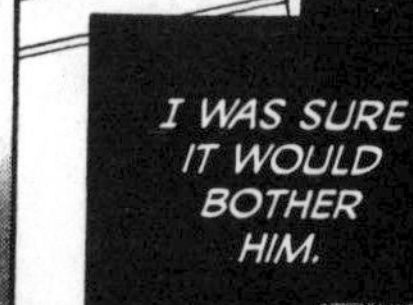

IF I SAID I WANTED TO STAY WITH HIM...
IF I WISHED IT...
I WAS SURE IT WOULD BOTHER HIM.
WITH HIS AWKWARD KINDNESS...
EVERY TIME OUR FEELINGS TOUCHED...
MY FEELINGS OVER-FLOWED...
BUT THE WORDS...
PIERCED MY HEART...
AND WOULDN'T COME OUT...

KEI-SAN WAS VERY...
FRIGHTENING.
BUT IT WASN'T HARD LIVING WITH HIM.
MAYBE IT WAS THAT KEI-SAN AND I WERE IN THE SAME DARKNESS.
HIS...
...PIERC-ING EYES...
...SEEMED TO CONDEMN MY WEAK-NESS.
BEING IN THE SAME SPACE...
...I BECAME EXTREMELY SENSITIVE TO HIS GESTURES.

AS DAYS AND MONTHS ADDED UP...

...LIKE THEY BELONGED TO JUST THE TWO OF US, WITH NOTHING CONNECTING US...

...CAME TRUE WHEN I MOST WANTED IT...

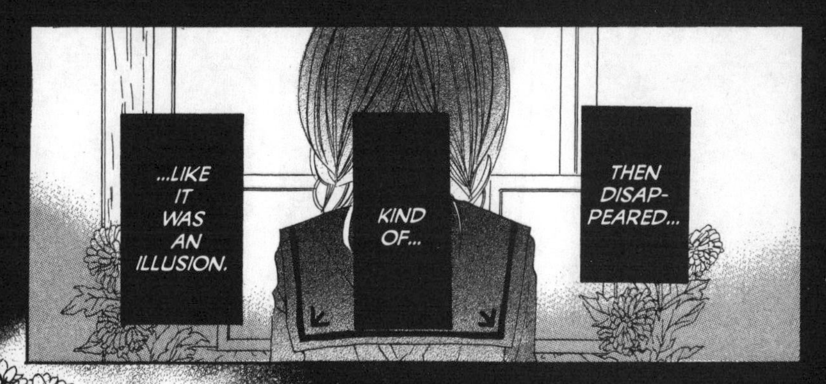

THEN DISAP-PEARED...
KIND OF...
...LIKE IT WAS AN ILLUSION.

THE REALITY THAT BORE INTO MY CHEST LOOKED LIKE A LANDSCAPE PAINTING.

AND, LIKE EVERYTHING WAS MELTING AWAY.

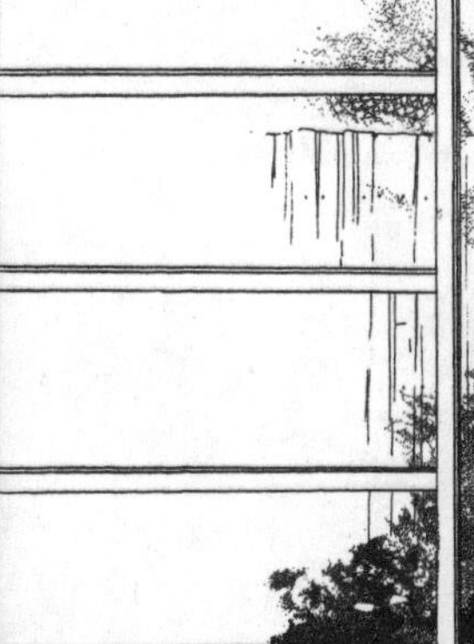

I LOVED MY GRAND-FATHER A LOT.
BUT HE WAS TWICE AS STRICT ABOUT HOME DISCIPLINE, AND, LIVING WITH HIM, I GOT THE FEELING I ALWAYS HAD TO SIT UP VERY STRAIGHT.
EVERY TIME...

I GOT A LETTER TELLING ME ABOUT THE FUN TIMES THEY WERE HAVING OVER THERE...
I FELT RELIEVED AND SAD.

AND MY WISH...

...AT THE TIME, I THOUGHT THAT IF I EVER SAID THE WORDS, "I'M LONELY," IT WOULD HURT THE PEOPLE I LOVED.

I SECRETLY DECIDED...

...THAT WHEN MY PARENTS GOT BACK, I WOULD ACT SO SPOILED THAT THEY WOULDN'T KNOW WHAT TO DO.

...BY THE TIME I HEARD ABOUT IT...

...THE ADULTS HAD ALREADY DECIDED ON SO MANY THINGS.
THEY TOLD ME I WOULD BE LIVING WITH MY GRANDFATHER UNTIL MY FATHER AND MOTHER CAME BACK.

MY FATHER ...
WOULD BE GOING TO AFRICA FOR BOTANICAL RESEARCH FOR FIVE TO TEN YEARS.
MY MOTHER WOULD BE JOINING HIM...
AND THEY WOULD LEAVE ME BEHIND.
THEY BOTH ...
RUFFLED MY HAIR...
AND SET OFF ON THEIR JOURNEY, CRYING.
BUT I COULDN'T EVEN GUESS...
...HOW FAR "AFRICA" ...
...OR "TEN YEARS" WAS.
AND I WATCHED THEM GO, WONDERING WHY.

花の名前
はな
な
まえ
The Name of the Flower
CHAPTER 13

MIZUSHIMA-SAN...
I...
...LOVE YOU.

DON'T YOU WANT TO PROTECT HER?
...I
...
I...
WOULD NEVER LEAVE YOU ALONE, MIZUSHIMA-SAN...
I WOULD STAY BY YOUR SIDE.
I...
WOULD NEVER MAKE YOU CRY...!

I'M SO...
WEAK.
I FEEL SO WRETCHED, I CAN'T STAND IT...
......
...I REALLY DID...
...THINK THAT SHE SMILES LIKE A FLOWER...
EVER SINCE THE TIME SHE FIRST SPOKE TO ME.
WHO DID THIS TO HER?
HOW CAN THEY MAKE HER SAY THESE THINGS?
SHE'S NOT EVEN CRYING, JUST TREMBLING.

LOOK...
EVERYONE HAS TIMES WHEN THINGS ARE HARD...
...AND THEY'RE AT THEIR WITS' END...!
NO.
...I WAS ONLY ...
...RUNNING AWAY...
...FROM THE SAME PAST.
LOOKING AWAY...
FROM THE SADNESS.
...SAYING I'M LONELY.

...
KARASAWA-SAN ...
DID YOU GET ANY REST?
YES.
THANK YOU.
NOT AT ALL.
UM.
I'M SORRY.
I woke you, didn't I?
AKIYAMA-SAN OWES ME FOR ALL OF THIS.
He went back to work.
I fixed the entrance and wiped the floor.
RUSTLE
RUSTLE
... WHAT'S ...?
OH.
This?
I JUST WENT TO THE CONVENIENCE STORE AND BOUGHT A BUNCH OF STUFF TO EAT.
Like yogurt, and water.
OHA-YO--
RUSTLE
ANYWAY, WHY DON'T YOU EAT AND GET SOME ENERGY?
RUSTLE
....
...
THANK YOU VERY MUCH.
...I
-- I'M SORRY YOU HAD TO SEE ME LIKE THAT.
THAT WAS DISGRACE-FUL...
IT WASN'T DIS-GRACEFUL!

I'LL BRING...
...KEI...
...TO YOU.
JUST YOU WAIT.
CLATTER
RUSTLE RUSTLE
HUH ...

...WANT TO BE ALONE ANYMORE ...
I'M SORRY.

NO MATTER HOW MUCH I WANT THEM, THEY GO AWAY SO FAST, AND NEVER COME BACK...
I DON'T KNOW WHAT TO DO.
...IT'S SO PAINFUL.
I CLOSE...
...MY EYES...
BUT IT STILL HURTS.
IT HURTS...
I'M SCARED.
I...
DON'T...

YOU'RE NO TROUBLE.
...
...
THEN...
PLEASE TELL ME THE TRUTH ...
WHERE ... IS ... KEI-SAN ...?
WILL ...
I EVER ...
SEE HIM AGAIN ...?
...I WON'T, WILL I?
CHOU ...
THAT'S HOW IT ALWAYS IS!

CHOUKO-
CHAN!
CHOUKO-
CHAN!
CHOUKO-
CHAN!
CHOUKO!!
WITCH
...AKIYAMA
...SAN.
ARE YOU OKAY?
AH,
YES...
...I'M SORRY TO HAVE TROUBLED YOU...

HEY ... IT'S NOT GOOD TO PLAY PRANKS, YOU KNOW.
BDMMMP!!
AAAHH! I'M SORRY!!
BDMP BDMP
I-IT'S YOU, AKIYAMA-SAN! WHY YOU!
WHAT ARE YOU DOING, KARASAWA-KUN?
NO,
UM...
MIZUSHIMA-SAN HASN'T BEEN TO CLASS FOR TWO DAYS...
I-I WAS WORRIED, SO I CAME TO CHECK ON HER...
BAM
EEHH !!??!
WH- WH-
WHY ...!!??!
STOMP
STOMP
And with his shoes !??!

CHAPTER 12, PART 2

AFTER THAT, WE STARTED TALKING ABOUT BLOOD TYPES, AND IT CAME UP THAT I'M BLOOD TYPE A, AND THE 100% FINAL BLOW WAS GIVEN TO ME IN THE WORDS, "PEOPLE WITH TYPE A DO GREAT WHEN THEY'RE WINNING, BUT ONCE THEY START TO LOSE, THEY GET WEAK." I STILL REMEMBER VIVIDLY SAYING, IN A VOICE LIKE A SOUL IN HELL, "THAT MAKES TWO OF US..."

My editor...  *Is type A, too.*

......
I NEED TO SEE CHOUKO-CHAN...
AND TELL HER ... EVERYTHING.
DING-DOOONG DING-DOOONG
DING-DOOONG
DING-DOOONG
DING-DOOONG
...
DING--

AMONGST THESE FLOWERS IN FULL BLOOM...
...WOULD BE SAVED.
THE DREAM-LIKE SCENE...
DAZZLED ME.
WHAT?
AND AGAIN, I...

AND THEN...
...I READ HANA.
AND MET "THE GIRL."
COULD I BELIEVE THIS?
MY MISTAKES FROM BEFORE...
MY MEANING-LESSNESS...
MY WORTH-LESSNESS
HAD ALL BEEN ERASED ...
IN THE TIME HE SPENT...
...WITH THIS GIRL WHO WAS SO CLOSE TO HIM.
KEI...

...AFTER I RAN AWAY...

...IORI LEFT KEI AND WENT TO STUDY ABROAD.
AS FOR KEI...
I HEARD HE QUIT...
...BOTH COLLEGE AND WRIT-ING...

A FEW YEARS LATER...
...WHEN HE WON THE NAOKI AWARD...

I SAW KEI FROM A DISTANCE.

HIS EYES SEEMED TO BELONG TO SOMEONE ELSE.

THEY WERE WEARY, MECHANICAL...

AND I COULD TELL THAT TO THOSE EYES, PEOPLE AND SCENERY WERE ALL EQUALLY EMPTY.

TO PROTECT MYSELF...
...I GAVE UP ON BEING INVOLVED.

AS HE CLUTCHED HIS KNEES AND BEGGED FOR FORGIVENESS...

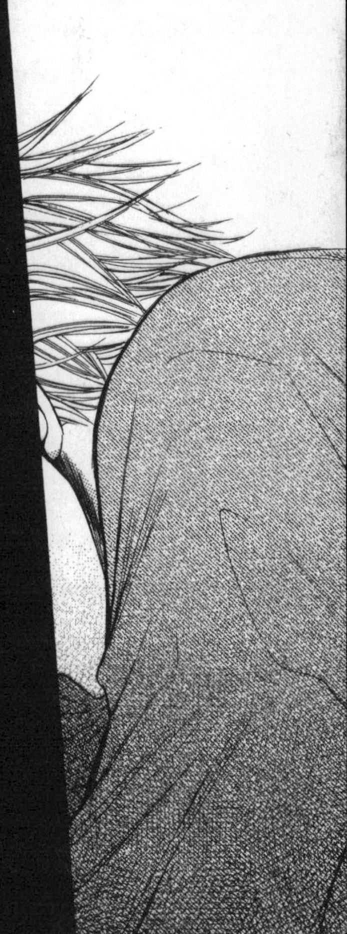

...I FELT AN INSANE SENSE OF SELF-SATISFACTION.

IN THE SLIPPERY HEAT...

S L O W L Y...

I BECAME EMPTY, AND BEFORE ME...

...KEI COWERED, HOLDING ON TO EVERYTHING ABOUT LIVING.

IT WAS UNBEARABLY BEAUTIFUL.

FOR THE FIRST TIME IN MY LIFE...

...I SAW THE DEPTHS OF THE DARKNESS IN SOMEONE'S HEART.

THE SUPERFICIAL WORDS...

...PEELED AWAY, LAYER BY LAYER.

I...

...WANT TO HELP YOU, KEI.

...THE HACKNEYED WORDS...

...THAT POURED FROM MY MOUTH.

I...

I THINK THE CICADAS WERE CRYING ENOUGH TO BURST.

MOTIVATED BY JEALOUSY AND HYPOCRISY, SET FOOT INTO DARKNESS.

I'LL STAY BY YOU UNTIL YOU GET BACK ON YOUR FEET, KEI.

...WHY KEI?

WHY IORI?

I, A SANE PERSON...

... KEI.
YOU OKAY?
I'M SURE YOU'RE JUST SICK.
WHAT'S SO PAINFUL?
WHAT'S MAKING YOU HURT? YOU'LL FEEL BETTER IF YOU TALK ABOUT IT.
TELL ME.
I'LL LISTEN, NO MATTER WHAT IT IS.
...
YOU ...
DON'T GET INVOLVED ...
NORMALLY...
DON'T SAY THAT...
I WOULD NEVER USE...

CAN'T TAKE MEDICINE.
WHEN HE REALLY LOOKS LIKE HE'S IN PAIN...
HE SAYS HE WISHES HE COULD DIE...
...BUT HE CAN'T.
HE SAYS HE WANTS...
...SUFFERING WORSE THAN DEATH.
THAT'S WHAT HE'S ALIVE FOR.
IT WASN'T IORI'S SMILE.
THIS MAN...
CLACK

HOW DO YOU KNOW WHERE IT IS, IORI...?
...HE'S THE ONE WHO INVITED ME.
IO--
COME ON.
COME WITH ME.
THAT STRANGE SMILE GAVE ME CHILLS.

CLATTER
SHIN-KUN.
I HEAR YOU WERE LOOKING FOR KEI MIZUSHIMA?
IORI...
DID YOU FIND HIM?
S-I-I-IGH
I THINK HE'S AT HIS HOUSE.
BUT ALL I KNOW IS THAT IT'S IN MITAKA...
...I KINDA GET THE FEELING I'LL NEVER SEE HIM AGAIN.
WANT ME TO TAKE YOU?
EH?
TO KEI'S HOUSE.
AND I DIDN'T NOTICE THE CHANGE IN IORI.

TEN YEARS AGO, I...
BROUGHT KEI AND IORI TOGETHER. A WHILE AFTER THAT...
...KEI STOPPED COMING TO SCHOOL.
IT LASTED TOO LONG FOR ONE OF HIS WRITING SPELLS.
I THOUGHT HE MIGHT HAVE JUST DROPPED OUT OF COLLEGE.
I PANICKED.
I WAS FRANTIC TO FIND OUT WHERE KEI WAS.

CHAPTER 12, PART 1

AROUND THIS TIME, THE MANUSCRIPT WASN'T DONE, I DIDN'T KNOW WHERE I WAS GOING TO MOVE TO, I HADN'T GONE TO MAKE MY FINAL REPORT; ALL THOSE PATHETIC REASONS HAD ME AT MY WITS' END MENTALLY, AND I COULDN'T SLEEP FOR A WHILE. WHEN I TOLD MY EDITOR ON THE PHONE, "I DON'T THINK I CAN GO ON ANYMORE...," I WAS TOLD, "YEAH, WHEN I HEARD YOUR VOICE, I THOUGHT, 'IS THIS PERSON OKAY?'" THEN, IN A REALLY CHEERFUL VOICE, "IT'S BECAUSE YOU'RE DRAWING SUCH A DEPRESSING MANGA!" THINKING ON IT NOW, IT WAS A BITTER MEMORY, IN A GOOD WAY.

ON TO PART 2

MURMUR MURMUR
YEAH.
MIZUSHIMA-SAN, RIGHT?
IT'S WEIRD. SHE'S ALMOST NEVER ABSENT.
SHE DIDN'T COME TO LINGUISTICS YESTERDAY, EITHER.
Man.
...
...SHE HASN'T COME TO THE CLUB ROOM, EITHER.
SINCE THAT DAY.
I HAVEN'T HEARD ANYTHING FROM OR ABOUT HER IN TWO DAYS.
IT'S TRUE THAT THAT'S NOT VERY LONG, BUT...
...BUT BACK THEN...
MIZUSHIMA-SAN SEEMED SO...
FRAGILE.

MURMUR
MURMUR
SHE'S NOT HERE?

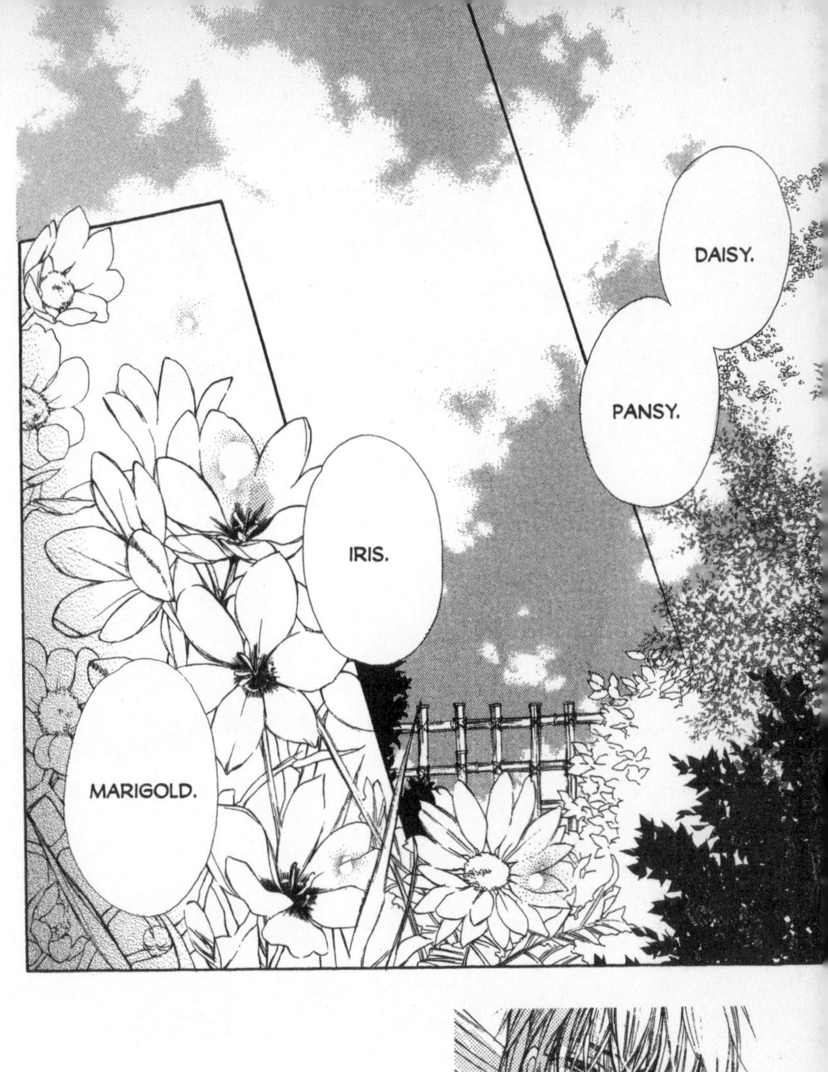
DAISY.
PANSY.
IRIS.
MARIGOLD.

花の名前
はな
まえ
The Name of the Flower
CHAPTER 12

MIZUSHIMA-SAN'S SMILE WAS LIKE A TREMBLE.
LIKE A SINGLE FLOWER, QUIVERING IN THE GLOOM.
IT WAS SUBLIMELY BEAUTIFUL ...
THE NAME OF THE FLOWER CHAPTER 11 / END

...
KARASAWA-SAN ...
IS SHE CRYING ...?
UH ... UM. UM.
I-IF YOU'RE NOT FEELING WELL, WE'LL...
NO.
I'M ALRIGHT.
BUT--
THANK YOU.
I'M FINE.

...I'M SORRY.
MIZUSHIMA-SAN.
WHAT IS SHE DOING IN THE DARK...?
M...!
She's in love with me. She's in love with me.
Erk!
CURSE
GET LOST, CURSE ...!!
AND HEY, WHY'D HE HAVE TO SAY THAT TO ME, ANYWAY! !??!
MOAN
That guy's such a jerk!
...
M--
MIZUSHIMA-SAN!
WHAT'S THE MATTER !!??!

EXCUSE ME.
WOULD YOU LET ME TALK TO HIM?
EH?
AKIYAMA-SAN...
CLATTER
HELLO ...
PLEASE!
......
CHOUKO-CHAN?
PLEASE LET ME TALK TO KEI-SAN ...!
......

YEAH!
MAYBE WE...
didn't give enough notice!!
ER, WELL THEN...
MAYBE WE'LL COME BACK LATER!!
AH...!
UM.
...
PLEASE DON'T LEAVE ...
...
TH-THEN...
DON'T MIND IF WE DO...
YES.
WH-WHAT DO WE DO?
CLATTER CLATTER
I TOLD YOU TO CALL BEFORE WE CAME ...!
What's with the heaviness!!??!
B-BUT, THE SURPRISE...!!
Weird. It shouldn't have been like this.
WHAT IS THIS?
...
ARE WE A GROUP WHO'S REALLY TERRIBLE AT GAUGING SITUATIONS ...!??!
I-I KNOW! LET'S CALL AKIYAMA-SAN!!
I got his number.
DA-KAP
DESPERATE
OH, THAT COULD WORK!
GOOD IDEA!! I'M SURE HE CAN GET RID OF THIS GLOOM!
WHAT'S THE MATTER ...?
Ah, hello, this is Katou.
OH, UM, WELL, WE'RE CALLING AKIYAMA-SAN...

...HAD ANY INTENTION OF BEING HAPPY.
DING-DOOONG
RATTLE
PARDON OUR INTRUSION!
TAISHO AUTHORS ASSOCIATION HERE!!
OH.
HELLO ...
EVERY-ONE ...
UM ...
IS THIS A BAD TIME?
OH, NO, KEI-SAN ISN'T HERE TODAY.
EH!??! REALLY !??!

DO YOU ...
KNOW SOME-ONE ...
WHO HAD THAT PROBLEM ...?
IT'S NOT A PROB-LEM
OF WHO HE WAS WITH ...
I DON'T ...
THINK KEI ...
EVER ...
CHOUKO-CHAN.

...
I SEE.
SO HE REALLY IS...
... AVOIDING ME ...
......
AKIYAMA-SAN.
WHEN WE PLAYED SHOGI THE OTHER DAY...
YOU SAID THAT THE MORE I LIKE KEI, THE HARDER IT WOULD BE.

AKIYAMA-SAN!
AH!
KEI-SAN ...
ISN'T WITH YOU?
PLEASE COME IN.
I'LL OPEN THE GATE...
NO...
HERE'S FINE.
... CHOUKO-CHAN.
KEI ...
MIGHT NOT COME HOME FOR A WHILE.

...GOT CARRIED AWAY, LIKE A FOOL.
I WANTED TO SHOW OFF--
KEI TO IORI...
AND IORI TO KEI.
KEI LOOKED SO SURPRISED...
I THOUGHT HE MIGHT BE SCARED.
IT'S POSSIBLE THAT IORI...
...?
LOOKED LIKE SOMEONE.
AT ANY RATE,
I SHOULDN'T HAVE INTRODUCED THEM.

BFF!
DON'T PLAY AROUND WITH WOMEN TOO MUCH!
Play with women!
WH-WHAT !??!
OH SHUT UP...
COUGH COUGH
ARE YOU ALL-RIGHT?
I'VE HEARD THINGS.
WHAT DID YOU COME TO COLLEGE FOR, STUPID!??!
"WHAT DID I COME HERE FOR" ...?
IF SHE FELT COMFORTABLE AROUND SOMEONE, SHE WOULD SMILE LIKE A CHILD.
DOES SHE KNOW HOW MUCH I HAD TO STUDY TO GET IN HERE?
Heh.
...ANYWAY, "KEI MIZUSHIMA."
TELL ME WHAT YOU REALLY THOUGHT.
IT WAS INTERESTING. I CAN SEE WHY YOU ALWAYS TALK ABOUT HIM.
I KNOW, RIGHT !??!
BACK THEN, I...

WHAT DID YOU THINK?
IT WAS LIKE LISTENING TO THE NIGHTMARES OF A CRAZY PERSON.
WHAT THE HECK?
HEE HEE.
IORI!
IORI TATEMATSU WAS MY CHILDHOOD FRIEND, A YEAR OLDER THAN ME.
READING'S ALL WELL AND GOOD, BUT MAKE SURE TO STUDY, TOO. OR YOU'LL MAKE YOUR UNCLE IN FUKUOKA MOURN.
I STUDY...
A FORMIDABLE WOMAN, WITH NO DISCERNIBLE FAULTS.
I'M JUST WORRIED. EVER SINCE WE WERE LITTLE, WHENEVER I LEAVE YOU ALONE, ALL YOU DO IS READ.
DON'T ACT LIKE YOU'RE MY BIG SISTER.
OH BY THE WAY, SHIN-KUN...

ABOUT HOW HIS PARENTS DIVORCED WHEN HE WAS VERY YOUNG...
HE LOST HIS MOTHER...
AND HE WAS LIVING ALONE IN THE HOUSE IN MITAKA THAT HIS GRANDFA-THER LEFT TO HIM WHEN HE DIED.
ABOUT HIS OLDER BROTHER THAT HE DOESN'T GET ALONG WITH.
ABOUT HOW HE CAN'T EAT SWEETS.
ABOUT THINGS THAT DIDN'T MATTER AT ALL.
KEI MIZUSHIMA...
TALKED GRUFFLY...
AS WE ATE TOGETHER.
I WAS SO HAPPY, I COULDN'T CONTAIN MYSELF.
SHIN-KUN.
PAT
I READ IT. "KEI MIZUSHIMA."

CHAPTER 11

I DID THE CHAPTER'S TITLE PAGE TO MATCH CHAPTER 10'S, BUT THEN THEY WERE IN SEPARATE VOLUMES. IT WAS A SHOCK. NOW NOBODY'S GOING TO NOTICE.
AROUND THIS TIME, I SPENT ABOUT TEN DAYS TRAVELING TO SPAIN.
IN SPAIN, I WAS IMPRESSED BY THE BUILDINGS OVERFLOWING WITH THE STYLE OF THE GENIUS ARCHITECT GAUDI , I CHOKED ON HOT CHOCO-LATE, I CRIED OVER THE CRUELTY OF THE BULLFIGHTING, I CRIED BECAUSE I JUST COULD NOT EAT ESCARGOT, AND I WAS KNOCKED OUT BY THE PASSIONATE FLAMENCO DANCING.
IT WAS FUN.

CLAMOR
Sure is crowded.
CLAMOR
A FEW MONTHS AFTER I STARTED TO NOTICE THE SUBTLE CHANGE IN KEI'S EXPRES-SIONS...
There are seats here!
CLATTER CLATTER
AH.
SOMEONE GOT THE SEAT NEXT TO KEI.
I'm too late!
... SORRY, BUT
THAT SEAT'S TAKEN.
Oh, I'm sorry ...
MURMUR
MURMUR
BUSTLE
... WHAT?
...YOU GIVE ME THE CREEPS ...
TOUCHED
Sit already.
OH ...
KEI
GRADUALLY STARTED TALKING TO ME.

WHEN HE WAS IN COLLEGE, HE WAS A NAMELESS NEW WRITER.
NEVERTHE-LESS, HE ALREADY HAD A FEW CORE READERS ON CAMPUS.
WHEN ANYONE GOT NEAR HIM...
NO MATTER THEIR INTENTION...
HE WOULD BRUSH THEM OFF LIKE INSECTS.
I PERSISTENTLY FOLLOWED KEI AROUND, NO MATTER HOW MANY TIMES HE BRUSHED ME OFF.
IN THE END, HE TREATED ME THE SAME AS HE DID THE AIR.
I DIDN'T CARE IF I WAS THE AIR OR WHAT...
I JUST VERY SELFISHLY, DESPER-ATELY...
WANTED TO TOUCH THE MIND OF KEI MIZUSHIMA.
I JUST KEPT TALKING TO HIM.
ABOUT ME...
...ABOUT LITERATURE...
ABOUT KEI'S WRITING.
HE USUALLY LOOKED FED UP WITH ME.
BUT SOMETIMES, LIKE WHEN I TALKED ABOUT LITERATURE, HE LISTENED, LIKE HE MIGHT BE INTERESTED.

WHOOOOSH
...KEI MIZUSHIMA.

JINGLE
YOU CAN RUN AWAY IF YOU WANT.
BECAUSE IT'S JUST LIKE WHAT HAPPENED TEN YEARS AGO.
YOU'VE SEEN IT, RIGHT?
THE LOOK ON HIS FACE...
...WHEN HE GROVELS BEFORE ME.

...YOU KNOW, SHIN-KUN.
I DIDN'T TAKE HIM AWAY.
KEI JUST FOLLOWED ME, ON HIS OWN.
I'M RENTING A PLACE FROM MY AUNT IN NERIMA.
I'M USUALLY OUT IN THE AFTERNOON.
HERE.
YOU CAN HAVE THIS, SHIN-KUN.
KEI HAS BEEN BROKEN FOR A LONG TIME.
YOU CAN GO SWEET-TALK HIM AS MUCH AS YOU WANT...
ANY TIME YOU WANT.
JANGLE!
YOU'RE SCARED, AREN'T YOU?

THAT MAN ...
HASN'T CHANGED A SINGLE BIT FROM BEFORE.
YOU'RE WRONG.
CREAK
NOW, KEI...
HAS A PLACE TO GO HOME TO.
YOU ABANDONED KEI.
PLEASE DON'T MESS THINGS UP NOW.
GIVE KEI BACK.
IORI.
JINGLE

HOW DID YOU KNOW?
OH.
I SEE.
HE'S THE MAN KEI USED TO LIVE WITH IN KYOTO.
HE SAID HE WAS THERE FOR HIM WHEN KEI'S MOTHER KILLED HERSELF.
... WHAT?
SHIN-KUN.
CREAK
I'M SURE THAT...
...IF I HADN'T READ *HANA*...
I WOULD NEVER HAVE SEEN HIM AGAIN, EITHER.
I WONDERED HOW HE WOULD LOOK AT ME AFTER WRITING THAT STORY. WHAT A JOKE.

CLUNK
HE WOULD CRY.
...WHAT THE HELL?
SAY, SHIN-KUN.
WHAT IS THIS "CHOUKO-CHAN" TO KEI?
HE TOOK HER IN AND IS RAISING HER?
WHAT A REPULSIVE MAN.
THEY'RE RELATED.
SHE LOST HE FAMILY WHEN SHE WAS IN HIGH SCHOO AND MOVED IN WITH KEI.
RELATED? TO KEI?
...HIS COUSIN'S DAUGHTER.
COUSIN?
YOH MIZUSHIMA?

YOU DIDN'T SEE HIM WHEN HE WON THE NAOKI?
IF IT HADN'T BEEN FOR *HANA*, I DON'T THINK I EVER WOULD HAVE GONE NEAR HIM AGAIN.
I WAS CRAZY NERVOUS WHEN I WENT TO KEI'S HOUSE.
...BUT HE...
...HADN'T CHANGED A BIT FROM BEFORE.
...IF YOU PRETENDED *YOU* FORGOT EVERYTHING AND WENT TO SEE HIM...
SHIN-KUN, THERE'S NO WAY KEI WOULD TURN YOU AWAY.
YOU'RE TALKING LIKE KEI'S IN LOVE WITH ME.
OH, COME ON, SHIN-KUN.
I'M SURE THAT IF *YOU* HATED KEI...

SO YOU'RE KEI'S EDITOR NOW?
YEAH.
I'M IMPRESSED.
WHAT DIRTY TRICK DID YOU PULL?
I DIDN'T PULL ANYTHING. HIS OLD EDITOR GOT SICK AND THEY PUT ME IN HIS PLACE. PURE COINCIDENCE.
I'M SURPRISED YOU COULD FACE HIM. AFTER LEAVING HIM THE WAY YOU DID.
...
I READ *HANA.*
I BET KEI WAS SURPRISED.
OH...
I WISH I COULD HAVE SEEN IT...
A better reunion than mine.
I *HAD* TOLD HIM THAT MY NAME WAS AKIYAMA ...
BUT IT WAS LIKE HE JUST COULDN'T BELIEVE IT WAS ME.
HE CHUCKED A DICTIONARY AT ME.
I thought I'd die.

SKID
N-NO,!
IT'S NOT WHAT YOU THINK! I-I'M... A FRIEND OF THE PEOPLE HERE!
IORI...! WHY ARE YOU HERE ...?
I THINK THEY'D HAUL YOU AWAY EVEN IF YOU WERE INNOCENT, SHIN-KUN.
THE GIRL YOU'RE LOOKING FOR ISN'T HOME YET.
WHAT ARE YOU DO-ING !??!
I'M STALKING A CUTE GIRL.
WHA --
SHE WAS TALKING TO SOME PLANTS IN THE GARDEN.
That was a sur-prise.
I SAW YOUR "CHOUKO-CHAN."
...
YOU'RE KIDDING.

GLANCE
GLANCE
SIGH
SIIIIIGH
......
GLANCE
GLANCE
...
WINCE!
HEY YOU!
WHAT ARE YOU DOING?!

WHEN I LEARNED THAT WE ATTENDED THE SAME COLLEGE ...
...I HAD TO GO SEE HIM. NOTHING COULD STOP ME.
KEI MIZUSHIMA ...
...WAS SO EXACTLY LIKE HIS NOVEL, IT SURPRISED ME.
HIS SHARP, INDEPENDENT EYES...
...MUST BE THE SOURCE OF HIS SPINNING OF WORDS THAT NO ONE COULD IMITATE.
I ADMIRED HIM SO MUCH I COULDN'T CONTAIN MYSELF.

FASCINATED BY THE BOLD, SURGING WORDS PAINTED BY THE LITERARY MASTERS ...
I'VE READ BOOKS, IMMERSED MYSELF IN THEM, SINCE I WAS LITTLE.
BUT IT WASN'T AS IF I HAD ANY LITERARY TALENT OF MY OWN.
AS THE DAYS PASSED ...
I BURIED MYSELF IN CONVERSATIONS WHERE "WORDS" MEANT NOTHING.
... AND THEN ...
...I READ KEI MIZUSHIMA'S BOOK.
A SCREAM?
A WISH?
THE STRING OF WORDS THAT WERE SO PAINSTAKINGLY CHOSEN ...
... FROZE MY SPINE ...
AND TOOK CONTROL OF MY ENTIRE BODY.

DIIIING
OH!
AKIYAMA-KUN.
BANDOU-SAN.
LEAVING ALREADY?
You cut your hair?
Yes, I did!
I HAVE SOMETHING TO TAKE CARE OF.
DIIIING
A WOMAN?
THAT'S RIGHT.
YOU'RE GOING TO MIZUSHIMA-SENSEI'S HOUSE, AREN'T YOU?
Seriously.
OH, HOW NICE.
GA-TANG
KA-CLANG
...I ALWAYS ...

......
...
...
PLEASE
...
DON'T WILT ANY MORE.

BE-CAUSE ...
YOU ...
"TREASURE" HER.
...BUT YOU HAVE NO INTENTION OF BEING SAVED.
CHIRP
CHIRP
FSSHHH
CLINK
CLINK

WHAT ARE YOU THINKING?
"CHOUKO-CHAN"?
YOU'RE A FOOL.

花の名前
はな
な
まえ
The Name of the Flower
CHAPTER 11

CONTENTS

The Name of the Flower

By Ken Saito

Volume 3